Use Opera

THOMAS ECCLESTONE

ISBN: **1503383725**
ISBN-13: **978-1503383722**

NONFICTION BOOKS BY AUTHOR

Celestia 1.6 Beginners Guide
Use LibreOffice Writer: A Beginners Guide
Use LibreOffice Impress:A Beginners Guide
Use LibreOffice Base: A Beginners Guide
Use Podio: To Manage A Small Company
Use Opera: The Internet Browser

CONTENTS

DEDICATION

This book is dedicated to my brother Simon for being a great man.

1 INSTALL OPERA

Some programs can still be quite difficult to install, but once you've downloaded it Opera is incredibly easy. Go to www.opera.com/download . It will detect the operating system and the version that you need to install automatically.

You'll see a large blue button that says Free Download then your operating system. When you click on it the program will start to download:

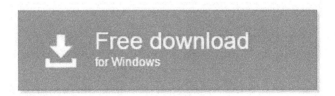

Your existing browser will show the download progress. For example, in chrome when you finish downloading you'll see a box at the bottom left hand corner of the chrome window with the file. Double click on it to run the executable.

Obviously each browser works slightly differently, but once it's finished downloading the file should be available in your downloads

directory by clicking on 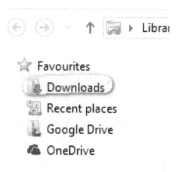 in the desktop view of windows, and then going to the downloads directory:

- Favourites
  - Downloads
  - Recent places
  - Google Drive
  - OneDrive

If you have a lot of files that you've downloaded, clicking on

Date modified should show the most recent download first. Double click on the file that contains Opera and then a version number:

Name	Date modified	Type	Size
Opera_25.0.1614.68_Setup	14/11/2014 13:57	Application	31,159 KB

This will start the Opera Installer dialogue. *You may have to click Yes on a User Account Control dialogue prior to the installer running, depending on your security set up.*

Once the installer is running you'll see a very simple window:

You can set some basic options such as where the program is to be installed to, the users that can run it, and the language. If you're happy with using the default Options you can simply click on:

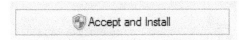

To run the installer. You'll notice that it is a very speedy process without any real human interaction necessary. The main Opera window will open once the installer is finished. You'll also notice the Opera button will be added to the task bar. You can click on it to open a new Opera window:

Install Options

If you want to change the installation options you can click on:

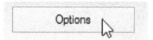

This allows you to:

- Select the language the Opera will use
- Choose whether to install it for global users or just the individual user and,
- Choose where to install it to.

Setting the Language

In the Installation dialogue click on the down arrow to produce a list of languages that Opera supports.

You'll normally find that the default language is the language that your operating system is set to use. So as a general rule the default option is the right one. But, nevertheless, you can choose from most popular languages in use today.

Changing the User

You can install Opera for all users on the computer (which is the recommended option) or for just the current user, or as a stand-alone installation. If you want to make an opera browser you can run from a USB pen you can use this option. If you do create a stand-alone installation I recommend changing the install path.

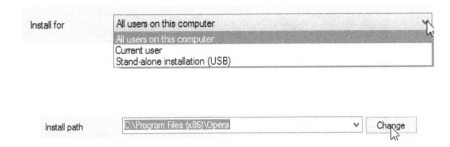

Changing the install path

The install path is displayed highlighted. For most purposes the default install path is fine, but if (for example) you want to install it on a network drive or usb pen you might want to change it. You can do this by clicking on Change:

This will display a Browse for folder which will contain the name of the main folders on your computer desktop

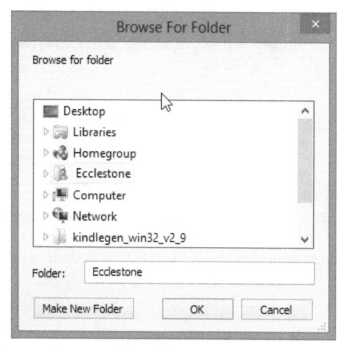

You can select an existing folder by double clicking on it, or you can make a new folder by clicking on the root folder,

then Make New Folder . You'll then have to type in the name of the folder (since you won't want it to be called "New Folder"

New folder by typing in the name you want and then pressing enter.

When you're happy with the options that you have selected press OK .

To run the installer using your selected options click on:

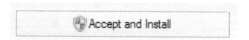

You'll notice that it is a very speedy process without any real human interaction necessary. The main Opera window will open once the installer is finished. You'll also notice the Opera button will be added to the task bar. You can click on it to open a new Opera window:

Opening Opera for the First Time

When you open Opera for the first time, right at the top of the screen there are two options that I suggest you choose.

Firstly, you can choose to make Opera your default browser. A default browser is the one that you use when you click on a link or URL in another application such as Microsoft word, or open a html file. It's a setting in your operating system.

I think that while you're still trying it out you should keep your existing browser as the default. You can change this setting later if you want, but I suggest that you click No:

The second option is whether you want to help improve Opera by sending usage information. This information is anonymised, but shows Opera if you have any problems, and allows Opera to know what parts of the program are most useful and therefore will get the most development time.

Personally, I clicked Yes on this option but if you have any security or data concerns you can easily choose not to participate by clicking on No.

Now we've installed Opera and dealt with some basic operations you can see the opening screen for Opera.

Opera Start Screen

The Opera Start screen can look a little intimidating at first, but it's very simple if you take it one element at a time.

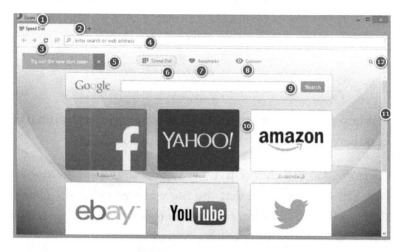

1. **Opera Button** Opera

    This Button shows a menu that allows you to access a lot of the tools and functionality of opera. It is like a menu bar, for example you can go to recently closed web pages, open up bookmarks, increase or decrease the size of the webpage (zoom), and several other useful features.

2. **Browsing Tab**

    The Browsing tabs allow you to quickly go from one web page to another.

3. **Quick Buttons (← Back, → Forward, ↻ Reload, ⊞ Start Screen)**

    These buttons allow you to go to the last webpage you were visiting (and then return to the current web page), refresh or reload the web page, or go to the start screen.

4. **Address or URL bar**

An address is something like

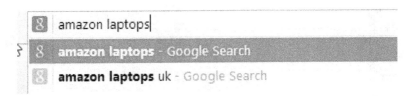 which directs you to a particular web site.

In the past you could only access information by typing an address, but now you can also type a search (for example a question or common word) into the box. A set of common suggestions will be displayed underneath. You can choose the one that relates to your search, or press enter.

When you type in an address and then press enter Opera will take you to the web site that you've typed in

5. New Start Page Button (optional)

Opera sometimes trials new Start Page layouts in an

effort to improve their search engine. It will display a New
Start Page Button on the start page if there is one that you
might want to trial.

At the time that I was writing the book, Opera was
trialling a new start page which looked like

Note that although the appearance is different (with
Speed Dial, Discover and Bookmarks on the left) the actual
functionality is all the same.

Like many search browsers the actual appearance of the
software can change, but as long as you understand how the
program works you normally find that it is pretty easy to
adapt.

You can return to the old start page by clicking on the
option at the bottom right hand corner of the screen.

6. Speed Dial button

Speed dial is functionality that allows you to open your most read webpages very quickly and easily. You can add web page tiles, remove them or move them about the screen easily.

Click on one of the tiles if you want to open the associated page.

7. Bookmarks Button

Bookmarks are like Speed dial tiles, but you often use them to organise web pages that you want to refer back to but may not use frequently. I'll discuss them in a future chapter.

8. Discover Button

This shows a page that you can use to find out the latest information and news on a variety of topics.

9. Search Bar

We've already seen that you can use the address and search bar to search whatever page you are on, but the Search bar is provided in the start page in order to give you direct access to google. Just type your search into the bar and you'll be able to find out about any topic

10. Speed Dial Sites

Clicking on a tile will automatically open up the associated web page. Each tile has the logo of the web page and the name of the web page beneath it.

Note that you can delete or move the tiles, or add new tiles, and I'll show you how to do these things later on.

11. Scroll Bar

This works the same way as with most applications. You can move the viewable area up or down by clicking and holding on the bar and moving the mouse up or down.

12. Search

If you move your mouse over Q you'll see a little search text field. If you click in the area that says

Search $\boxed{Q\ Search \qquad\qquad I}$ you can type in a site that you've saved in bookmarks or the Speed Dial and it will be brought up:

Going to your first Web Site via a URL / Web Address

Click in the URL / Web Address bad at the top of the screen (number 4 above)

Type in the web address that you want to go to. For example, the BBC news web address is http://news.bbc.co.uk

Press enter.

Notice that while you're loading up the web page you'll see a little wheel logo appear on the tab bar for the tab that you are open on. You'll also see the name of the web site.

Once the site has finished loading you'll see it appear in the main viewable area – the area that was originally the start page.

Connection Errors

Note also that you may have an error like the following if your internet isn't connected:

If you haven't connected to the internet, then you can often do so by clicking on the logo at the bottom right hand corner of the screen. Sometimes, if you have too many buttons you may have to click to show the internet connection box.

Make sure that flight mode isn't on, and that you double click on the connection that you want to establish. You may need to type in a password or similar. You can use the operating system help to find out more methods of troubleshooting if you can't get the internet connection to work.

Next Chapter

In this chapter I've described how to install opera and go to your first web site.

In the next chapter I'm going to describe the basic features of Opera. At the end of the chapter you should be able to visit most web sites.

2 USING OPERA TO VISIT WEB SITES

Going between web pages

There are two main ways that you can use to navigate the internet:

- **Web Addresses**
- **Web links.**

Web Addresses

You type web addresses directly into the address bar. They often look like http://google.co.uk or http://yahoo.co.uk .

When you use a web address it will general be because you've visited the web site numerous times, or you've been told the address by someone.

Understanding Addresses

An address consists of a domain (and subdomain) and a file location.

Domain names are names that the internet uses to locate a

particular site. They are divided into three or four main sections i.e. before the double slash there is a format (http) which is technical information that the web browser needs to use to fetch the file. *Opera generally assumes that a website will use http:// unless you specify otherwise, so you don't have to type this section of the domain name.*

Then there is actual domain name (which may include subdomains , google is a domain name, the news in news.bbc is a subdomain).

When you start a web site most people purchase a domain name from a domain registrar. The company makes it possible for your computer to locate a specific domain on the internet.

The domain followed by a domain level such as .co.uk which identifies the country or the subject of the domain. .co.uk is a British country, .gov.uk is a British government site etc.

This all sounds pretty complicated, doesn't it? But most of these details just become automatic. Ultimately you just type in the address for the site, you don't need to know what it means. The knowledge can help you a little because if you have accidentally typed in the wrong address it can be easier to spot that you've got the format wrong.

Not needing to remember addresses

It would be a little cumbersome if you could only navigate using web addresses. Who wants to type out the full address every time you want to go to a page?

There are two pieces of functionality in Opera that store web addresses for you. These are Speed Dial tiles and Bookmarks.

You can also go to specific sites called search engines which are special sites that are used to find information or subjects that are useful to you.

In this book we repeatedly go to google.co.uk (there are other google sites such as google.com which is the American google version, google.fr for google France and dozens or even hundreds more).

Web Links

A web link it something that the web developer (the guy or lady who wrote the web page) puts into a web page to enable you to go to another web page that it references.

In the early days of the internet a link was generally just a piece of blue text that was underlined when you hovered your mouse over it. When you clicked it, you'd go to another site. It still appears that way on, for example, google.

Link - Wikipedia, the free encyclopedia
en.wikipedia.org/wiki/**Link** ▾
Jump to Computing and **Internet** - [edit]. **Links** (programming language), a web application programming language that presents an alternative to the usual ...
Link (The Legend of Zelda) - Hyperlink - Data link - Satellite link

Note that when your mouse is over a link it also changes to the hand icon . This is a very useful sign that you're over a link.

Look at the bottom left hand corner of the screen while you are over the link. You'll see the address that you'll navigate to if you click on the link.

en.wikipedia.org/wiki/Hyperlink

Warning: it is often wise to check that the address of the link that you are about to click is reasonable. I.e. the domain name looks right (a trusted site like Wikipedia.org, google, yahoo etc. that you are familiar with rather than a string of odd letters and numbers) and goes to the site that you want to go to.

It's not impossible for an address to be a spoof, and if you click on an address which goes to the wrong place you might even end up infected with a virus.

When you click on the link you'll end up at a new web page.

Image Links

Sometimes, links can be embedded in images or in animated graphics such as flash or JavaScript. You can tell that an image is a link by hovering the mouse over it. The cursor will change to a hand shape if the image is a link. You'll be able to click on it, and go to another web site.

Embedded Video

When you click on a video link in a site like youtube.co.uk the video should automatically start loading. Often you see a buffering signal such as ![buffering icon]. Don't worry if you see such a sign – the browser is just storing enough data to run the video smoothly.

Making a web page smaller or larger

If you have bad eyes sometimes it is hard to see what the web page is displaying. Or maybe you have a picture that is larger than the screen you're using.

It's easy to make the web page smaller or larger by zooming.

First click on the ![Opera button] button at the top left hand corner of the screen.

You'll see the Zoom option.

Zoom   ‹   100%   ›   ↕

Click on the left arrow to make the page smaller:

And the right arrow to make it larger:

Note that you can reset the zoom to 100% (i.e. normal size) by clicking on ⟨⟩ .

Full Screen Mode

Sometimes even using the zoom functionality doesn't give you the best web browsing experience. When you want to see as much of the web page as possible either press F11 or click the ⟨Opera⟩ button and hover your mouse over page. Then click Full screen.

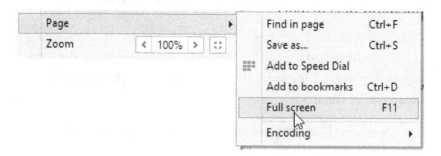

You'll see that the menu bar, and everything except for the web page that you are viewing will disappear.

For example, this is Google in full screen mode:

Note that you don't see any of the browser functionality at all. You'll need to press the escape key (often top left hand corner of the keyboard labelled esc) in order to return to the normal viewing mode.

Private Browsing Windows

A lot of people are concerned about being able to use the internet in privacy. Opera provides a basic amount of privacy by using Private Windows.

When you close a Private Window all the data that Opera has used or stored is immediately removed. For example:

- Cookies (files that contain information about your identity)
- Temporary files
- Browsing history.

This provides a basic amount of privacy but if you download a file it may still be available in your downloads folder, and often you'll find that internet sites record a lot of data about you which they store in their own site and servers and which Opera can't prevent them recording once you've given it to them.

If you are very concerned about privacy it is important to use more complicated methods than available under Opera to maintain that privacy.

You can start a private window by clicking on the 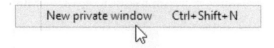 button to get the Opera menu. Then click on New Private Window.

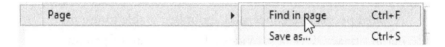

Find Text in a Page

Sometimes when you have a large web page you might want to find a specific text phrase.

To do this click on the 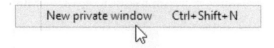 button, then hover your mouse over page.

Then click on Find in page:

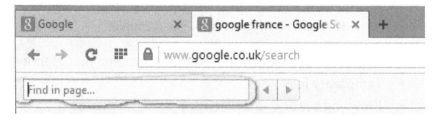

You'll see a find box appear at the top of the web page

Type in the text that you want to find:

You'll see that the text is highlighted through the page:

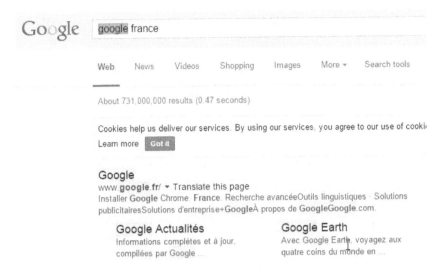

Note that the current instance (i.e. where you are) is highlighted in green, the others are highlighted in yellow. You can click on

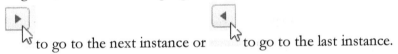

to go to the next instance or to go to the last instance.

You can see how many items you've found to the right hand side

of the arrows.

Using multiple Web Pages at once

One of the advantages of Opera is that its tabbed interface allows you to use a number of web pages at the same time. At the top of the page, under the opera browser you can see the tabs that you've got open. In this example there is only one tab (google) open.

Open a tab

You can open a new tabby clicking on besides the current tab.

Note that when you do this, the tab opens on the speed dial page:

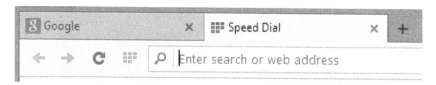

You can select one of the speed dial options, or you can type in an address.

Switching between tabs

To go between tabs you can simply click on the tab that you want to look at. In this example you've got the Google tab open and you're about to click on the Amazon tab.

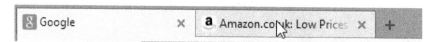

One thing that people sometimes don't notice is that if you hover your mouse over a tab without clicking on it Opera produces a preview that shows what is on the web page.

Closing a Tab

Once you've finished with a tab, click on the cross by its name.

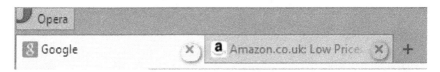

Note that if you close the last opened tab, Opera doesn't shut down. Instead it opens a new tab at the speed dial window.

Reopening the last closed tab

Sometimes you may close a tab accidentally. This can be very irritating. To reopen the last tab you closed right click on the area to the right of the + symbol in the tab bar

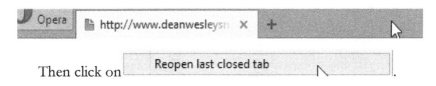

Then click on [Reopen last closed tab].

Reopening other recently closed web pages

To reopen other recently closed web pages click on the [Opera] button.

Hover your mouse over Recently Closed to see a list of the tabs that you have most recently closed. Then click on the one that you want to open again.

Cloning a Tab

Sometimes you might want to switch between different views of the same web page. You can do this by cloning a tab – which means creating a new tab with the same address / web page as an original tab.

Right click on the tab that you want to clone, then click on:

You'll see a duplicate tab appear.

Note that when you scroll in one tab it doesn't have an effect on any other tab.

Pinning a Tab

Sometimes you may want to prevent a tab from being accidentally closed. Simply right click on the tab that you want to remain open and press 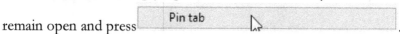 .

Notice that the tab will become smaller on the tab bar:

You can still click on it to open it up. Pinning tabs is often used when you have a web chat session so you don't accidentally close it.

To unpin a tab right click on it and

select  .

Save a Tab to Speed Dial

Sometimes you may want to go to a page so often that you want to add it to your speed dial tiles. I don't recommend doing this very often. Only do it to sites you'll visit every day.

Right click on the tab then click

on 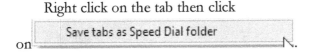 .

Undocking Tabs (Moving Tabs to their own window)

When you're working with several tabs and want to have a tab in its own window it's pretty easy to undock it by hovering your mouse over the tab, clicking and holding the left mouse button and moving the tab onto the desktop.

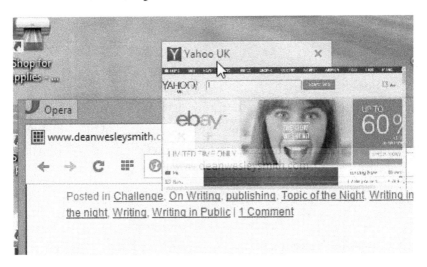

You can dock a tab (i.e. move a tab onto another window) by left clicking on it, and moving it over the plus on the tab bar and then letting go.

Note that you can also move a tab in the tab bar by holding on it and moving is to the left or right. This can be useful when you have a lot of tabs open and want to keep the ones that you are refering to most frequently in the same place.

Bookmarks

A bookmark is a way for you to store web addresses that you may want to go back to at some future date. While you can keep the most frequently used web locations in the Speed Dial tiles you've already seen you'll often find that it isn't practical to keep too many locations in Speed Dial.

Adding a Page to Bookmarks

To add a page to your bookmarks click on the heart next to the web address in the address bar.

You'll see the heart go red, and a preview of the page to be bookmarked appear below the heart.

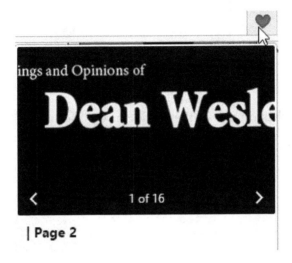

Sorting Bookmarks

All bookmarks start off as unsorted bookmarks when you add them. This is a bit like just shoving the bookmark in a random draw. It's important to sort bookmarks into the proper files when you make them. When you use the internet for months or even years at a time you often find that you can get hundreds or thousands of bookmarks!

So it's important that you look below the preview and click on the down arrow next to Unsorted Bookmarks

If you've already got the folder that you want, you can simply click on it. By default there are four bookmark folders:

If you click on one of these folders you'll see under the bookmark preview, the location will be the new folder:

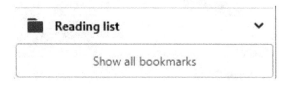

Adding a new Bookmark Folder

Sometimes you may want to add a new file to your bookmarks list. You can do this by clicking the down arrow next to Unsorted bookmarks

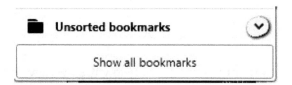

And then clicking on the plus besides New Folder

You'll see the text New Folder being highlighted

Type in the name of the folder

When you press enter you'll see that the bookmark has been added to the new folder automatically.

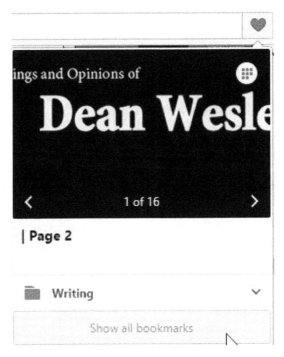

Also, when sorting bookmarks you'll be able to see the new folder you just created in the list of folders that you can assign the bookmark to.

Adding Bookmarks to the Bookmarks Bar

In the same way you have the speed dial functionality there is also a bookmarks bar which allows you very rapid access to a limited number of sites.

When sorting a bookmark, click on

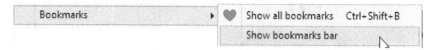 Bookmarks bar

. which is at the bottom of the list of bookmark folders.

To show the bookmarks bar

First click on the Opera button.

Hover your mouse over bookmarks then click show bookmarks bar.

You'll see the bookmarks bar appear under the address / search bar.

Note that clicking on a bookmark on the bar will automatically open the web page that the bookmark belongs to.

To hide the bookmarks bar

First click on the Opera button.

Hover your mouse over bookmarks then click show bookmarks bar.

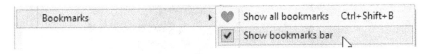

Show all bookmarks

First click on the  button.

Hover your mouse over bookmarks then click on Show all bookmarks

This will open a new tab, which contains the bookmarks page.

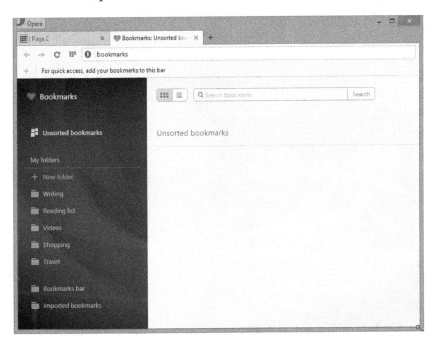

Note that on the left hand side there are folders, and on the right hand side are the bookmarks you've currently stored in the folder.

Click on one of the folders under my folders:

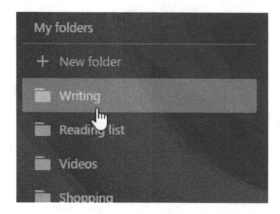

And you'll see that the bookmarks on the right hand side frame will change to the bookmarks that you have stored in that folder:

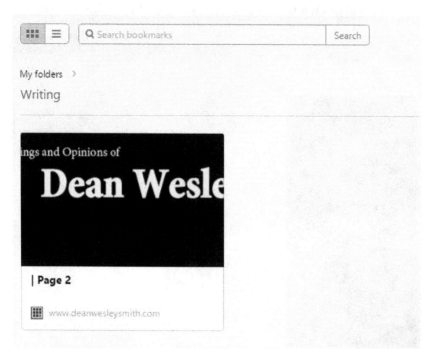

Search bookmarks

At the top of the bookmarks folder there is a little search bar that you can use to search for bookmarks.

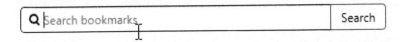

Type the text that you want to search for:

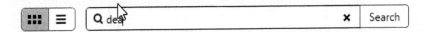

As you search any bookmarks that much the text of the bookmark that you are interested in will be displayed below the search bar.

Tile or List Bookmarks

By default Opera shows tiles for bookmarks. The tiles show a preview of the site, so you can easily see which bookmark is the one that you want to use. But sometimes, after you've been using Opera for a while, you have so many bookmarks in a folder that the Tile view can be very cumbersome.

You can get around this by clicking on the Toggle list view icon to the left hand side of the search bar.

This shows the bookmarks as a list

Sorting Bookmarks in the Bookmarks Page

If you want to move a bookmark from one folder to another

you can either open the bookmark and use the method shown in Sorting Bookmarks above or you can click and hold on the bookmark and then drag it over the folder on the left hand side frame. Let go when the bookmark is over the correct folder.

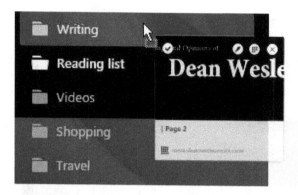

Opera Turbo Mode

Sometimes you may want to speed up browsing, for example if you have a bad internet connection. Opera provides functionality that does make a difference when you are browsing many sites called Turbo Mode.

Using Turbo mode automatically compresses and shrinks part of a web page that you don't need to see in Opera's cloud before you download the web site. It does this by analysing the site that you are about to visit before starting to download.

Because you're downloading much less data you'll actually find that the web sites that you use suddenly take much less time to download.

Opera doesn't use Turbo mode on sites that are secure such as bank sites, or email or any other web page that uses the https:// format (i.e. any page that is encrypted)

To turn on the Turbo Mode click click on the button.

Then click on .

If at any point you want to turn Opera Turbo mode off go back to the Opera menu by clicking on the Opera button and then click on ✔ Opera Turbo for a second time.

I really do recommend always using Turbo Mode, though, since I find that it is one of Opera's best features.

Printing a Web Page

When you are working on the internet you will often want to print a web page out. Before opening the print dialogue choose whether you want to print the entire page out or only part of the page. If you want to print part of the page highlight that part using a mouse.

Then bring up the Print dialogue by going to the Opera menu by clicking on the Opera button.

and pressing .

You'll see the Print Dialogue open.

Choosing a Printer.

Opera automatically selects your default printer, but sometimes you may want to change to another printer.

At the top of the dialogue there is a list of printers that your system is using. The default printer is highlighted. Click on whichever printer you want to use.

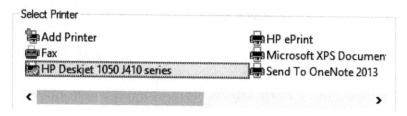

If you don't see the printer that you want to use click

on  .

This will open a dialogue showing any network printers you have. Choose the one that you want in the normal way.

Printer Preferences

Opera gives you the ability to change a number of things about the way that your document prints.

Click on Preferences to open these preferences.

Firstly you can change the Orientation from portrait (upright) to landscape (sideways)

You can also change whether it prints the first page last (i.e. your printer reverses the order of the print out so that you have it in the correct order).

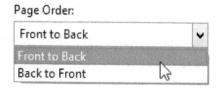

Some people also want to automatically shrink documents to 50% or less, so you have more than one document on a page

As a rule with this option I think that no more than 2 pages per sheet on A4 paper is wise.

I.e. if you are using A3 paper you might want to use 4 or 9.

These basic preferences are good enough for most people, but you may also want to also change a few other things that affect how Opera prints out the document.Click on Advanced... .

You'll see a dialogue with a lot of underlined preferences. To change a preference click on the underlined portion.

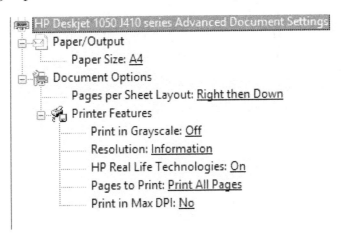

For example to change it so you only print in black and white to save money click on the word Off:

Print in Grayscale: Off)

And choose Black Ink Only (the cheapest option), or High

Quality Grayscale.

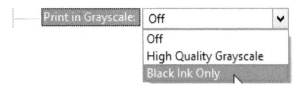

Once you're happy with your choices in the advanced menu click

on ⬚OK⬚ . Also click ⬚OK⬚ in the preference

dialogue if you're happy with the selections you made there.

Choosing how many copies to print

To print more than one copy of the document you need to click into the Number of Copies text box and change the number 1 to the

amount of copies [Number of copies: 1] . You can also click on the

up and down buttons by the box if you want increment or decrement the number.

Choosing what parts of the document to Print

The parts of the document that you want to print can be determined using the Page range section.

By default, Opera prints out the entire document.

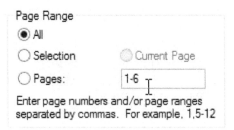

If you want to print out a selection that you highlighted earlier,

click on ⭘ Selection .

Or you might want to print out a particular range of pages, in which case click on ○ Pages: _____ then put in the range of pages you want into the box ● Pages: | 1,2,3-6 | .

Note that you can separate page ranges:

- 1-3 will print out pages 1, 2, and 3.
- 1 will print out page 1
- 1,2,3 will print out pages 1,2,3
- 1,2-3 will print out pages 1,2,3
- **1,1-3 will print out pages 1,1,2,3**
- 1,3-4 will print out pages 1,3,4

Note that each range is separate, so if you have the same page in multiple ranges it'll print it out twice.

Before you print

I generally suggest that before you print you look at the pages section to check how many pages you're printing. Sometimes a web page might be very long indeed, and you'll end up printing out dozens or even hundreds of pages.

The last number in the Pages section tells you how many pages the document contains.

○ Pages: | 1-6 |

Note that this doesn't work very well if you are printing a selection, but presumably if you do that you know how many pages you are likely to print.

To print the pages you have selected press | Print | .

Save Page

Sometimes you may want to save a page to your local computer.

You can save a web page by clicking on the 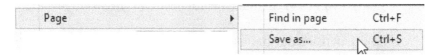 button to open the Opera menu, then hovering your mouse over Page and clicking on Save as.

This will open up a save dialogue which you can use in the ordinary way. One thing to note is that the save as type might look a little unusual:

Save as type: Webpage, Complete

You can choose to save everything in the web page (web Page, Complete) which includes images and generally most of the web pages. Or you can choose to store only the HTML.

When you save a web page you need to be aware that many web pages depend on dynamic content i.e. information that the web page creates on the fly. These web pages may not display correctly when you open them later on.

Please note: Copyright law varies depending on jurisdiction. Before saving or using a web page make sure that it is legal for you to do so in your country.

History

Sometimes you may want to find out what web sites you have viewed. Or simply go to a web site that you visited yesterday, or even weeks ago.

You can view your website history by clicking on the 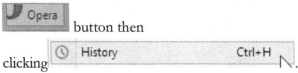 button then clicking .

You will see a web page with a list of sites that you have visited:

Note that on the left hand side there is a list of links that you can click to determine how old the sites displayed will be. For example, the default is that you are showing all links, but you can show links from today, yesterday, a week or a month too.

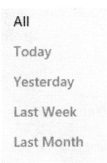

There's also a search button. Type in the word (or part of a word) that you want to search your history for. Opera will show a preview of sites that match your selection:

Note that when you are searching you can click on

Exit search to return to the main history page.

Each of the page addresses in the history is a link, so if you hover your mouse over it the pointer will change to a hand shape and the text will become underlined:

Today - Thursday, 20 November 2014

10:55 ▦ http://www.bbc.co.uk/news/ - www.bbc.co.uk

Like all links, clicking it will open the web page.

Clearing History, Cookies, and other data

You can always prevent Opera from recording history data by going into private mode. But say you haven't done that and you want to remove the history data from your computer. You might also want to remove cookies which are bits of data that a website uses to identify your or store information about your choices on your computer.

You can do this from the History page which you visited in the last section by clicking on the Opera button then clicking History   Ctrl+H.

On the top right hand side of the screen you'll see Clear browsing data... . Click on it to open the clear browser data dialogue.

The two important sections of this dialogue are the section that determines which part of your history data to delete. Click on the time frame to choose whether to delete data from the last hour, last day, week, and month or from the start.

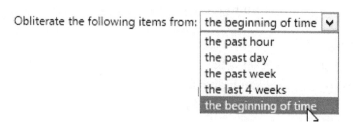

Then there is a section that determines what data you want to delete.

☑ Clear browsing history
☑ Clear download history
☑ Delete cookies and other site data
☑ Empty the cache
☐ Clear saved passwords
☐ Clear saved Autofill form data

Note that Browsing history is the list of web pages that you have visited, download history is the list of files that you have downloaded, delete cookies removes information that other sites stores about your identity and your preferences in using their sites, empty the cache deletes temporary files and files like images that your browser stores to make sure that your computer browser runs more quickly.

By default clear saved passwords isn't checked – this option will remove password data that you store so you can access sites more easily.

And it also doesn't check autofill data – this is data like names, addresses and URL that you often want to use again and again.

Once you are happy you can click Clear browsing data to complete the data clearance. Note that this is a permanent choice – once you've deleted the data it's not possible to recover without specialist tools and techniques used by experts.

Note also that, on its own, clearing browser history isn't going to remove all traces of the internet sites you've visited as far as a determined expert is concerned. It'll clear your history for casual users but not for the police. [And if you want to find out how to do that, you'll have to get another book ☺] As a rule it's better not to go to sites that are illegal anyway.

Next Chapter

In this chapter I've shown you some of the basic functionality of Opera. This includes ways to speed up your browsing, go to sites, print out websites, and use various methods to store websites that you have visited in the past.

In the next chapter I'm going to talk about how to use a common web search engine (google.co.uk) to find pages that you are interested in.

3 SEARCHING

In this chapter I'm going to give you a brief tutorial in how to use a common search engine available on the internet to find web pages, images, news stories and even shopping items that you are interested in.

This chapter isn't intended to give you every detail about how to use search engines. You could write an entire book on that. It's just intended to give you a good start.

Searching google from the address and search bar

While you can run a google search just from the search bar, such as the example below:

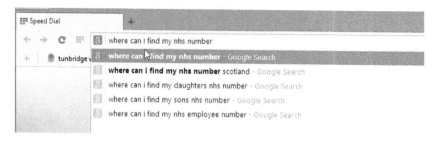

One thing that people often don't notice is that Opera produces a list of predictions about what you're likely to search for below the text:

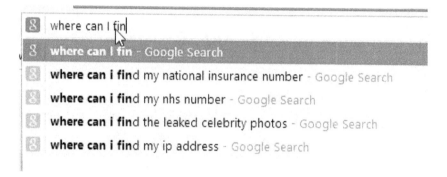

This is often scarily accurate. If google predicts a question that you want answered, simply click on the link. Otherwise type in the full question you want answered:

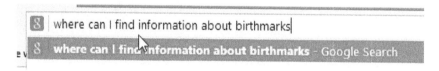

Going to Google Directly

You can also go to google directly by typing the address into the address or search bar:

Keywords versus Plain Text

Originally the best way to search google was to use something called "Keywords" and you'll see people still doing this. For example, say you wanted to answer the question:

How many people are born with birthmarks?

Keywords are words that you'd imagine to be the most common search terms for the subject. So you might type:

Into the search bar. You imagine that medical epidemiology is better than the English language version of the query. Thinking in terms of keywords can still be useful. What language would someone who was writing about your subject use in their webpage?

The above query produces the following answers:

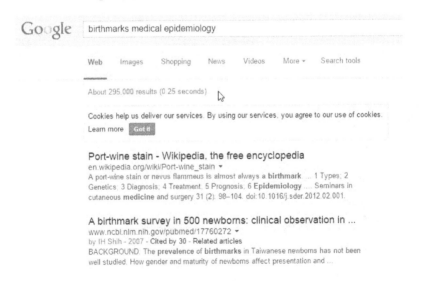

So it is a pretty good answer to the question.

Note that on first impressions the original question doesn't produce results that are quite as good:

Google | How many people are born with birthmarks?

Web   Images   Shopping   News   Videos   More ▾   Search tools

About 478,000 results (0.39 seconds)

Cookies help us deliver our services. By using our services, you agree to our use of cooki
Learn more   Got it

Birthmark - Wikipedia, the free encyclopedia
en.wikipedia.org/wiki/**Birthmark** ▾
A **birthmark** is a benign irregularity on the skin which is present at birth or ... as light
brown in fair-skinned **people**, to almost black in darker-skinned **people**. ... may be
present at birth, or appear in early childhood, and do not fade much with age.
Café au lait spot - Mongolian spot - Congenital melanocytic nevus

What are birthmarks? - Medical News Today
www.medicalnewstoday.com/articles/174886.php ▾
★★★★☆ Rating: 4 - 10 votes
26 Sep 2014 - Some people are born with pigmented **birthmarks**; these are usually ...

But if you click on the first link you also get information that answers your question.

Keywords are still a very useful tool when searching for a particular topic but it's often worth just asking google the English language question you're interested in now. Google can often work out the best webpage to show you without your having to work as hard.

Defining a word

Google allows you to find out the meaning of a word. Just type in define and then the word you want to define in the search bar:

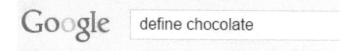

You'll see the definition appear once you hit enter:

chocolate

/ˈtʃɒk(ə)lət/ ◀))

noun

a food in the form of a paste or solid block made from roas·
seeds, typically sweetened and eaten as confectionery.
"a bar of chocolate"

- a sweet made of or covered with chocolate.
plural noun: **chocolates**
"a box of chocolates"

- hot chocolate.

Click on ◀)) to hear the word spoken.

Converting from one unit to another

Use the phrase x unit in unit to convert from one unit to another

Produces

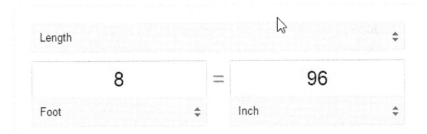

Or

Produces:

Note in the above example that google automatically converts an imperial fraction (like pounds) into a metric quantity before completing the conversion.

While google doesn't automatically convert into imperial fractional measurements, if you type in

It will send you to a site that will help to answer your question!

Searching a specific site

Sometimes you may want to search a specific site for information rather than the whole internet. For example, you may want to search a forum site like moneysavingexpert.com which has huge amounts of information on a specific topic rather than wanting results from all over the internet.

Google has operators that control how and what you are searching. One of these is the site: operator. Using site: and then the internet site that you want to search will restrict the search to only one internet site. (Note, there must be no space between site: and the site that you want to search)

Google | site:bbc.co.uk gold

Produces only results from the BBC:

Web   Images   News   Videos   Shopping   More ▾   Search tools

About 290,000 results (0.26 seconds)

Cookies help us deliver our services. By using our services, you agree to our use of cookies.
Learn more Got it

In the news

Bangladesh Biman airline 'gold smugglers' arrested
BBC News - 23 hours ago
In recent months, **gold** smuggling in Bangladesh has increased significantly. Customs ...

Ex-serviceman Matt Richardson makes Para-skeleton history
BBC Sport - 2 days ago

More news for site:bbc.co.uk gold

Sites that link to a specific site

You can use the Link operator to search for sites that link to a specific page:

Google | link:deanwesleysmith.com

Note that the above example only shows links to the homepage. If you want to show links to a specific web page within a web site you'd need to use the address for that site.

Show sites similar to a web page that you already know

The related: keyword is useful if you want to show sites that are like a site that you already know.

Google `related:bbc.co.uk`

Produces a list like:

The Telegraph - Telegraph online, Daily Telegraph, Sunday ...
www.telegraph.co.uk/ ▾
Latest news, business, sport, comment, lifestyle and culture from the Daily Telegraph and Sunday Telegraph newspapers and video from Telegraph TV.

Al Jazeera English - Live US, Europe, Middle East, Asia ...
www.aljazeera.com/ ▾
Aljazeera.com: Latest Video News Updates from US, Europe, Middle East, Asia-Pacific and Africa. Watch Live Weather Updates, Business and Sports News.

Reuters.com: Business & Financial News, Breaking US ...
www.reuters.com/ ▾

Search Operators

There are a number of operators that you can use to specify more thoroughly what information you want to search for. You can find a long list of them at https://support.google.com/websearch/answer/2466433?hl=en (since they do regularly change) but the most common ones are the OR operator, the " " operator and the – operator.

Using Or in search

Say you want a Nikon or a Fuji DLR camera

Google `nikon or fuji camera`

Will tend to bring up pages that either compare Nikon or Fuji cameras, or pictures that contain the word Nikon or the word Fuji.

Not searching for specific words

If you want to prevent google from searching for a specific word use the – operator

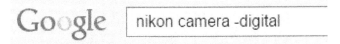

Will search for pages that contain the words Nikon camera but don't contain the word digital.

Searching for words in a specific order

You can use the " "operator to search for a phrase that contains the words you are searching for in a specific order

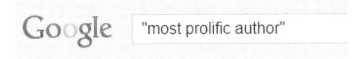

Produces web pages that match that specific search term:

Despite his position as the world's most prolific author, **Sverker Johansson** hasn't lost his Swedish sense of self-deprecation. "Well, three million articles is hard to beat but, you know, a lot of them are quite boring.

The world's most prolific writer - Features – N by Norwegian
www.norwegian.com/magazine/features/.../the-worlds-most-prolific-writer

 Feedback

List of prolific writers - Wikipedia, the free encyclopedia
en.wikipedia.org/wiki/List_of_prolific_writers ▾
Philip M. Parker, by one measure the world's **most prolific author**, has an entirely different approach. Parker has over 200,000 titles listed on Amazon.com, ...

Henry Anatole Grunwald: Simenon - World's Most Prolific ...
www.trussel.com/maig/life58.htm ▾
An all-Simenon Library receives another volume as the author and his wife add new copy of Le Président to shelves in their chateau. Library contains only ...

The most prolific author you've never heard of » MobyLives
www.mhpbooks.com/the-**most-prolific-author**-youve-never-heard-of/ ▾
22 Jan 2014 Meet Craig Osso, aka Russell Blake, a retired American property

Using google to search for products

Say you are searching google for Nikon cameras:

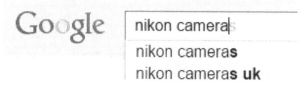

When you click enter you'll see a web page containing search results for Nikon cameras.

These days Google is actually a range of different search engines. If you specifically want to search for products, click on the shopping link just below the search bar.

Web   Shopping   Images   News   Videos   More ▾   Search tools

Will show a list of products to you including the prices:

Web   Images   Maps   **Shopping**   More ▾

Digital Cameras › Nikon   Sort: Default ▾   View: List ▾   ■ My Sho
                                                                        Merchant links are sp

Most popular

Nikon D5100 16.2 MP Digital SLR **Camera** - Black - AF-S VR DX 18-...
£299.99 from 10+ shops
★★★★★ 54 product reviews #1 in Nikon Digital Cameras
April 2011 · Nikon · SLR · Crop Sensor · 16.2 megapixel · 3 x optical zoom · Pop-up Flash ·
Detachable Flash · 560 gram · CMOS
Other lens bundle options: AF-S DX 18-105mm VR lens (£385) More

Nikon D800 36.3 MP Digital SLR **Camera** - Body only
£1,516.99 from 10+ shops
#2 in Nikon Digital Cameras
Nikon · SLR · 36.3 megapixel · Pop-up Flash · Detachable Flash · 900 gram · Body Only · CMOS

Changing the filters for Product Search

Note that no the left hand side of the screen there are filters,

58

including location. You can click on change to change the location you are searching from:

Crowborough, UK
Change

You can also specify only new products New items by clicking on the square, and other options such as price range etc.

Shopping for the Product

Click on the link below a product

Most popular

Nikon D5100 16.2 MP Digital SLR Camera - Black - AF-S VR DX 18-...
£299.99 from 10+ shops
★★★★★ 54 product reviews [#1] in Nikon Digital Cameras
April 2011 · Nikon · SLR · Crop Sensor · 16.2 megapixel · 3 x optical zoom · Pop-up Flash
Detachable Flash · 560 gram · CMOS
Other lens bundle options: AF-S DX 18-105mm VR lens (£385) More

You'll bring up a page on the product. You can read peoples reviews by clicking on the reviews link next to the

star ★★★★★ 54 product reviews

Or scroll down to see the list of shops it is available from:

Sponsored (5)

Sellers ▾	Seller Rating	Details	Base Price	Total Price	
SLRHut	★★★★★ (1.519)	Free shipping	£299.99	£299.99	Shop
MobiCity UK	★★★★★ (1.229)		£362.39 +£4.99 shipping	£367.38	Shop
eGlobal Central UK	★★★★☆ (217)	Free shipping	£291.99	£291.99	Shop
eBay - lee262onlineuk	No rating	Free shipping	£301.00	£301.00	Shop

Click on the Shop button to go to that shop.

Using Google to Search For Images

Once you've typed in the item that you want to search for, click on Images in the search tool links below the search bar:

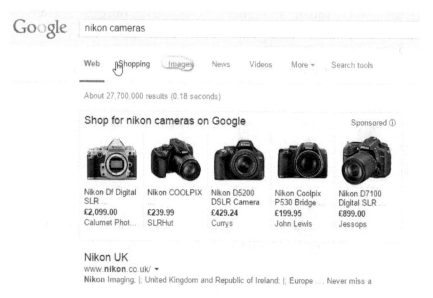

This will bring up google image search

Note that this page can vary a little depending on if it's a product brand or some other item. A product brand may have lines below the search:

Which you can use to get particular product lines.

Whereas a search for something like wellington boots may have common types of wellington boots:

Getting Public Domain images

To search for images that are only in the public domain click

on Search tools .

This provides a number of search tools that you can use to filter the images that you are searching for. Click on Usage Rights:

Size ▾   Color ▾   Type ▾   Time ▾   Usage rights ▾   More tools ▾

This will bring up a number of usage rights. For example, if you can reuse it with modification (including commercial) or only reuse it, or if it's only available for non-commercial use.

Note that if you do this it doesn't absolutely guarantee that you're within the terms of the law. You must still check what terms you need to abide by for the reuse to be legitimate. For example, you may need to attribute the original owner or provide any modified version for free.

Other Filters

Using Search tools (above) you can filter the image by the dominant colour, size, type (i.e. line drawing, cartoon, photograph etc.), and when the image was uploaded.

Downloading an Image

Obviously firstly you must make sure that you are downloading the file legally, i.e. that you have the right legal permissions (see above) to download it.

Then go to the image in the google search and click on it.

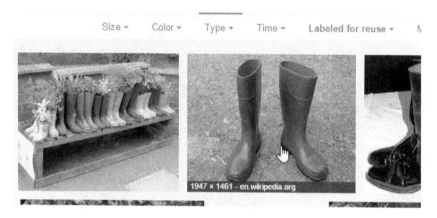

This will bring up a large version of the picture

Click on 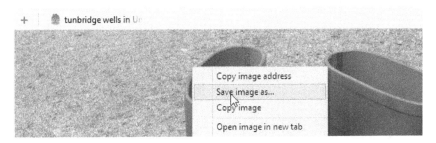. This will bring up the highest resolution version of the image that google has.

Right click on the image and then click on Save Image as

This will bring a save as dialogue which you use in the normal way.

Opera will show the download progress

And the file will be stored to the folder that you chose in the file dialogue. Often this will be your downloads folder.

You can see a file that you have downloaded by clicking on the **Opera** button to get the Opera menu. Then click on 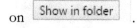 .

You'll see the Downloads page open up with a list of files you've downloaded today, and in the past.

The list includes the location of the image, and where you've stored it. You can open the image by clicking on **Open** or you can show the image in the folder where you caved it by clicking on **Show in folder** .

Note that on the left hand side is a frame that allows you to show completed, paused, and active downloads. And you can search downloads if necessary in the same way you'd search browser history.

Using Google to search for Videos

After typing in the search, click on Videos in the list of search engine tools.

Wellington Boot Repair with Stormsure Adhesive - YouTube

www.youtube.com/watch?v=XUqkbukOhQ4 ▾
5 Feb 2010 - Uploaded by Robert Altham
Repair leaks in your **Wellington boots**. A leak, split or perished
▶ 2:02 rubber will ruin your day. Not any more! Use ...

How wellington boots are made - YouTube

www.youtube.com/watch?v=780DsKqsHP0 ▾
29 Sep 2012 - Uploaded by John Alston
See the work that goes into making a pair of wellie **boots** by
▶ 3:42 Novesta ! To find our more or buy a pair visit the ...

This will bring up a list of videos.

You can filter the search by clicking on   Search tools   which
allows you to filter the duration of the video, when it was uploaded
(using any time) the quality and where in the world the video was
uploaded (using the web)

The web ▾   Any duration ▾   Any time ▾   Any quality ▾   All videos ▾   Any source ▾

Watching the video

Click on the video that you want to watch. The video will load,
and then start playing when it has buffered enough to produce a
decent image.

You can pause the image by clicking ▌▌ then start it again by pressing ▶. Pressing ⌜ ⌝⌞ ⌟ makes the video full screen. Press escape (esc on the top left of most keyboards) to go back to normal view.

Note that sites other than youtube may work slightly differently. Google does have image search for sites other that youtube (which is the largest video streaming site in the world, and which google owns) but they work in a similar way.

Using Google Maps

So far we've used google to find out information, to search for products, images and videos. But a very useful tool with google is google maps. This gives you the ability to search for physical locations.

Say we wanted to find out the location of a railway station, we'd type the name into the search bar

 tonbridge railway station

And then click Maps .

You'd then see a map of Tonbridge highlighting the railway station.

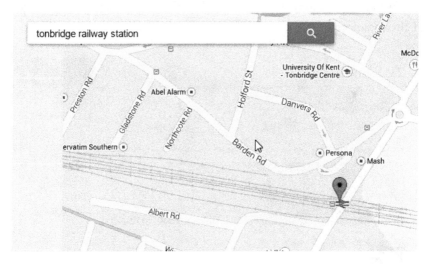

You can also type in addresses such as:

25 southfield road tn4 9uh

Which will display a map

Where you search for locations like this you'll also get a picture of the location

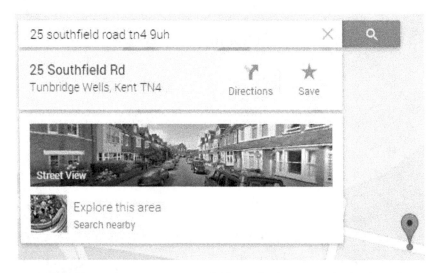

This allows you to get a good idea of what a particular location looks like.

Getting Directions

You can get directions by using the search START ADDRESS to DESTINATION ADDRESS

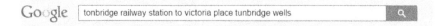

You get a map like this

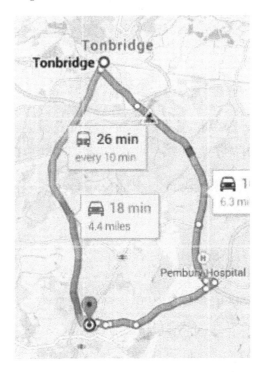

You can choose another route by clicking on the grey line.

Note that you get a street map that often relates to the road journey, but by clicking on  for car, for bus or public transportation, or for walking or for bike you can choose other methods of transport. Hover your mouse under the transport type:

And you'll see the option to list the steps that you need to take in order to make the journey.

I admit that I've only covered the most basic facilities of google maps, which can include things like showing you the next time for bus journeys if you click on ⬛ . But I think that I've given you enough to be getting on with.

Next Chapter

In this chapter I've covered the basics of search.

The next chapter will cover how to set up and use a Gmail account for internet email. This will allow you to send email to anyone for free to anyone whose address you know.

It'll also allow you to receive email yourself

4 HOW TO USE GMAIL

.

In this chapter I'm going to show you how to use the most popular web-based email program in America, google mail. I'll show you how to sign up for a new email address, and I'll also show you the basic methods you need to use to send mail, attach documents, download documents and read email.

Sign Up for a Google Account
If you already have a Google Account you can skip this step

While I could give you the direct link, I think it's sensible to start with a search to revise the last chapter. So, in your address / search bar type

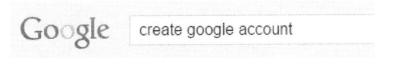

The first result should be create google account. Click on it:

Create your Google Account

accounts.google.com/Signup ▼

A single username and password gets you into everything Google (Gmail, Chrome, YouTube, Google Maps). Set up your profile and preferences just the way …

You'll be taken to a web page with "Create your user account".

Fill in the form, i.e. your name

Name

Tom	Ecclestone

You email address. This is the email address that you will use when accessing google services. It has to be unique, i.e. if you try to type in an email address that someone else has you'll get this error:

Choose your username

tomecc   @gmail.com

I prefer to use my current email address

Someone already has that username. Try another?

Available: ecclestonetom   tomecc65
tomecclestone999

You just need to try email addresses until you have a unique one that you are happy with.

Note, everyone else will be able to see your email address so make sure that it's one that you can live with!

When you create your password google will automatically assess how good it is. You want to use a password that is quite long, and preferably also uses letters and characters.

	Create a password
Password strength: Too short	.. I
Use at least 8 characters. Don't use a password from another site or something too obvious like your pet's name. Why?	**Confirm your password**

Password tip: it's important to create a password that you can remember. Lots of people decide to use single words, birthdates, or the names of a pet. These things are all stored in password cracker applications and make it exceedingly easy for a hacker to get into your account.

One of the best ways to make a secure password is to use a phrase like 'ilovebritneyspears' or 'sausagedogsarecool' which is very easy to remember but very difficult for a hacker to guess.

Once you've got a password you're happy with you'll unfortunately have to type it in again.

Then add your birthday, gender, and so on as google asks you.

Validation email: Google will ask you for an email address. If you have one, put it in. If you don't you'll have to leave this blank.

Phone number: If you have a mobile phone I generally advise adding it here. This allows password recovery as well as adding extra features.

There's something interesting here, called a captcha. This is a piece of text or a question that is intended to make it harder for someone to program a computer to automatically enter data into a web page. It prevents spamming. Type in the text.

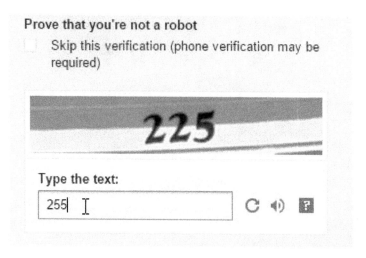

If you can't read the text press 🔊 so that google reads it for you.

You need to put in your location and then click the box to agree to the Google Terms of Service

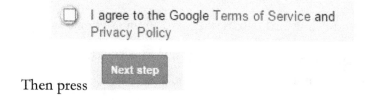

Then press **Next step**

Account Verification

I'm going to assume that most people who are using this chapter don't have an email account already. If you do have an email then google will send a verification email to the account that you entered during sign up. Simply click the link in the email and you've verified your account.

Otherwise you'll do a phone verification.

Google will send a text to your phone and you'll enter the code in the text:

Verifying your account

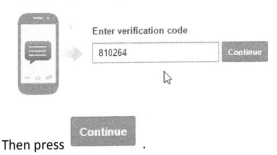

Then press **Continue** .

Create a Profile

The next scree that you see will allow you to create a google+ profile. This is effectively a public web page that allows people to see some of your details. You may want to add one later, but at the moment

you don't need to. So press No, thanks .

Your New Email Address

Google will display a new email address. It is important that you either write down or remember your email address and your password. You'll need this every time you start Gmail

Welcome!

Your new email address is ecclestonetom@gmail.com

Signing into your Google Account

The first step in using Gmail is to sign into your google account.

To sign into your google account type Google's web address into the search bar

Then click on **Sign in** at the top right hand corner.

Google will take you to a page which has your email address (note, if the email address is wrong then click

on Sign in with a different account) and a space for a password. Type in your password

Please re-enter your password

ecclestonetom@gmail.com

Password

Sign in

Need help?

Sign in with a different account

Google may ask you for information on recovery email addresses and phone numbers. You can either add this information and click **Done** or choose to ignore it and

click No thanks . As a rule it's a good idea to make sure that you have at least a recovery address or phone number otherwise you can lose access to the account.

Once you've signed in you'll return to the main google page. One thing will be different. At the top right hand corner of the screen you'll see your email address:

+You   Gmail   Images   ⣿   ecclestonetom@gmail.com ▾

Log in to Gmail

Once you've signed into your account to open up Gmail click on it at the top right hand corner

+You   Gmail   Images   ⣿   ecclestonetom@gmail.com ▾

It'll take a little while to load the first time

Loading ecclestonetom@gmail.com...

The first time you open Gmail you may see a splash screen like:

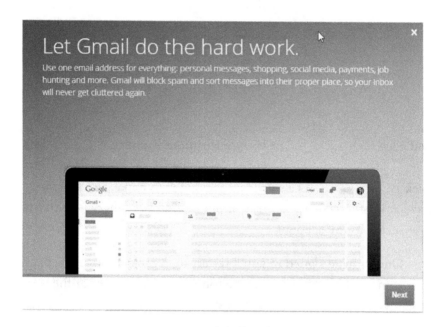

Read the message then Click .

The final screen will say something like

ecclestonetom@gmail.com is ready to use.

Go to Gmail

Click Go to Gmail .

Your Inbox

The new Gmail screen may look a little intimidating, but the first thing you want to do with it is look at the emails that are waiting for you … and that's pretty simple.

The first screen you'll see when you open Gmail for the first time is the inbox screen. This shows emails that are waiting for you in your 'inbox'.

Each line shows information about an email. To select an email click on ☐ to the left of the email. Ignore the star for now. The next email is the address or name of the person who sent you the email. In this case, Gmail Team.

The next column shows the subject of the email:

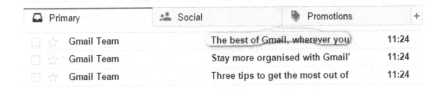

Finally, there is the date or time the email was sent.

Read an Email

To open an email you can hover your mouse over the subject line

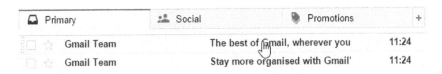

Notice that the subject line is a link, so the mouse pointer changes to a hand icon. Press the mouse button.

You'll see the email open.

Email Header

At the top of the email is the header. This contains the subject:

And the folder the email is currently stored in (this is the inbox at the moment) Inbox x .

Plus who sent you the email, and when:

Gmail Team <mail-noreply@google.   11:24 (28 minutes ago)
to me

You can print out an email by clicking 🖨 .

Email Text

Below the header is the text of the email. Read it, and if it doesn't fit into the screen scroll down until you've read the end.

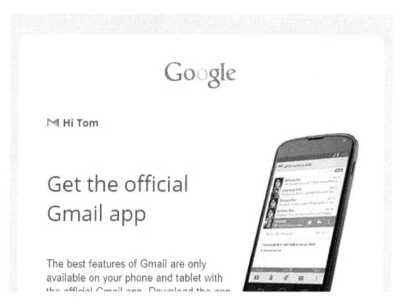

Read the Next Email

Notice that once you've read an email you have a number of options. You can click on next at the top right hand corner of the screen to read the next email in the folder:

Return to the Inbox

You can return to the inbox by hovering your mouse over inbox on the left hand side of the screen and clicking inbox:

Email Maintenance Options

Above the email header is a toolbar of maintenance options. You can use these options to delete, report an email as spam.

Delete an Email

If you've read an email and are satisfied that you won't want to reply to it or need to read it again you can delete it by

clicking 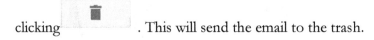 . This will send the email to the trash.

To Report an Email as Spam

If you think that an email is unwanted you can report it as spam

by clicking  .

The effect of this is that it not just removes the email but prevents that sender (or messages that are very similar to messages that you've reported as spam) going directly to you. They go to your spam folder instead.

To Archive an Email

Sometimes you may want to archive an email. This means that google will store the email but you won't see it in your inbox. You'll be able to access it later on if you want to.

To do this click

Archive an Email into a Category

So far we've just dealt with emails in the inbox. But you'll often find that if you just leave your emails in the inbox they'll become a complete disorganised mess.

One of the most basic ways to organise an email is to have different categories that you can archive your emails into. For example, you may have folders for business functions (recruitment, HR, accounting) or projects.

To move an email to a category you can click on and then click on the category which you want to move it to. There are some basic categories that have already been created, including social, promotions, updates, and forums

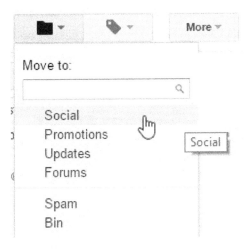

Here's the thing: by default when you've read an email and moved it to a category it disappears from the inbox. Even when you click on the category tab:

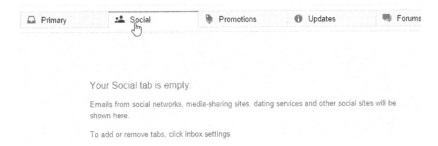

You won't see anything.

You'll see the emails you've just moved by doing a search on the category:

But because you've dealt with them they're not in the inbox any more. They're archived.

Showing Items in a Category

You can show items in a category by clicking on the more option under compose

Then clicking on the category that you want to show

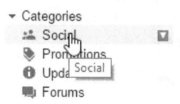

This will show emails in the category

Adding New Categories

While Gmail has a number of default categories it is often very useful to create new categories. You can do this by clicking

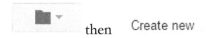 then Create new .

This will bring up the New Label dialogue. You can type in the label name

New Label

Please enter a new label name:

☐ Nest label under:

Choose a label to nest under (i.e. Project-> Use Opera) if necessary by clicking on the check box ☐ Nest label under: and then choosing the appropriate category from the list.

Once you're happy click Create .

The email will automatically be archived to the category.

Categorising Emails in the Inbox

Sometimes you may want to put emails into categories without actually archiving them. Gmail offers the ability to categorise posts within the inbox so that you can still read an email without doing a category search.

You can do this by using the labelling functionality in Gmail.

To Label an Email

First select the email in the Inbox by clicking on the ☐ .

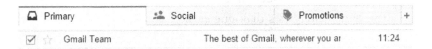

Then press the label icon  to produce a list of current labels:

Click on the labels that you want to apply. You can add more than one label to each email.

Click   Apply   .

You will see a message that says which labels you've assigned the email to.

The conversation has been added to "Social","Forums". Learn more Undo

Adding a New Label

Select the email as above. Then press the label icon and press: Create new   .

You'll see a New Label dialogue which will work in the same way as the New Categories dialogue earlier.

Writing Email

So far we've shown how to read and manage an Email. Now, to get the most out of Gmail it's important to learn how to send email to someone else's email address.

There are two main scenarios where you'll send an email:

- **Composing an email, where you start a conversation.**
- **Replying to someone else's email.**

Both situations are very similar, but you'll sometimes find that during a conversation (i.e. emails on the same topic to the same person) you may end up doing both. You compose an email to someone else, they reply, and then you reply to the response.

Composing an Email

The first step is to press the **COMPOSE** button while you are in your inbox.

This will bring up the New Message Dialogue:

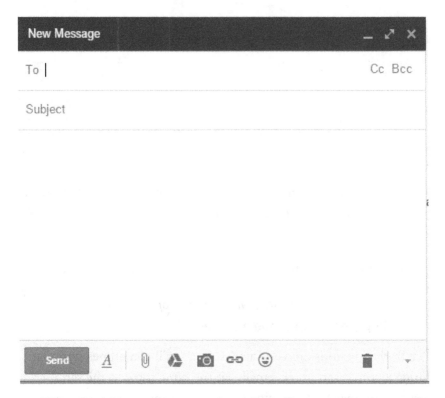

When looking at this we see that it's similar to reading an email. You have your header, which contains a TO: address and a subject (as well as two other forms of addresses, Cc and Bcc).

Then you have the Message body.

Below the Message Body there is a list of options that allow you to add links, formatting, and pictures.

Adding a To: address

The first field you have to enter is the To: address. This is the primary email address of the person that you want to contact. Note that you can send an email to more than one person, but we'll cover that later.

Type in the email address into the box

To thomasecclestone@yahoo.co.uk| provided.

Note that with email addresses the format is always very similar... you have a particular name, followed by the @ symbol, followed by a domain and the domain type (i.e. .co.uk in this case).

Adding Other Email Addresses

Sometimes you may want to send an email to more than one person. If this is the case you have two options:

- Add a CC address. This means 'Carbon Copy' from the old days of office memos. With a CC address everyone knows that you've emailed that person.
- Add a BCC address. Or a 'Blind Carbon Copy' which means that you'll hide the fact that you've emailed the person.

As a general courtesy, if you are emailing a lot of people that may not know each other's email address it is polite to use a BCC since you don't want anyone to end up having their email address used by spammers (by people that send unwanted email).

BCC's can also be used for less generous purposes - I'm sure the office politics options are almost unlimited!

To add a CC address click on Cc . Then type in the address:

Cc random@anywhere.co.uk

To add a BCC address click on Bcc then type in the address:

Bcc itswrong@nowhere.co.uk|

Note that when you add a TO, CC, or BCC address and press enter a box forms around it:

Bcc itswrong@nowhere.co.uk ✖

And to remove the address you have to click on the cross ✖ .

There's another thing you'll notice. thomasecclestone@yahoo.co.uk is a real email address. random@anywhere.co.uk itswrong@nowhere.co.uk are fake real addresses. Gmail accepts all three because they are all in legitimate email format. Gmail will try to send the emails, then send you an error message to say the latter two email addresses couldn't be delivered to.

You'll see the emails listed at the top of the screen after you've entered them and moved onto the next field.

To change the addresses hover the mouse over the line with the email addresses you've just entered.

Adding a Subject

To add a subject to your email click onto

Subject

And then type whatever subject line that you want.

Press the tab key or click into the next box to add your main message.

Adding a Message

Once you've added the subject line and pressed tab you'll be in the main message window. Just type in whatever message you want to send.

In essence, that's it. At least if you only want to send a basic message to your contact. However, you can improve the look of your email using text formatting options, adding photographs, and add links.

Text Formatting

Highlight the part of the text that you want to format.

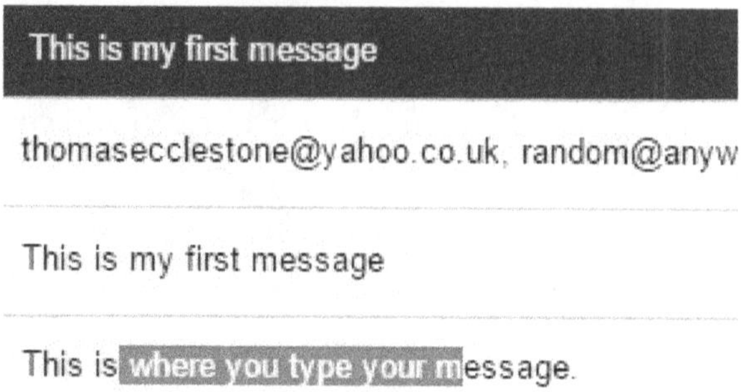

This is my first message

thomasecclestone@yahoo.co.uk, random@anyw

This is my first message

This is where you type your message.

At the bottom next to the send button is the text formatting icon $\underline{A}$. Click on it.

You'll see a range of text options appear.

The first option is the font. Currently you've got a Sans Serif font. If you click on 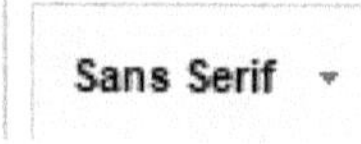 Sans Serif ▾ you'll see a list of fonts that you can use:

- ✓ Sans Serif
- Serif
- Fixed Width
- **Wide**
- Narrow
- Comic Sans MS
- Garamond
- Georgia
- Tahoma
- Trebuchet MS
- Verdana

Sans Serif ▾

Click on the font that you want and you'll see the text that you highlighted changed. For example, click on wide

To make the text that you've selected wide font.

This is where you type your message.

To increase or decrease the size of the font click on ᴛT ▾ .

B makes it bold, *I* makes it italic, U̲ makes it underlined, A ▾ is used to change the text or the text background colour, ≣ ▾ to change the allignment so that the text is left, centre or right aligned or justified. ≣ for a numbered list, ≣ for a bullet point list.

You can indent the text using ≣ or decrease the indentation by clicking on ≣ .

Attaching a file

When you want to send a file to someone else you can attach it to an email. For example, when you want to send a report you've written to your boss. To attach a file click on 🖉.

This brings up a file open dialogue:

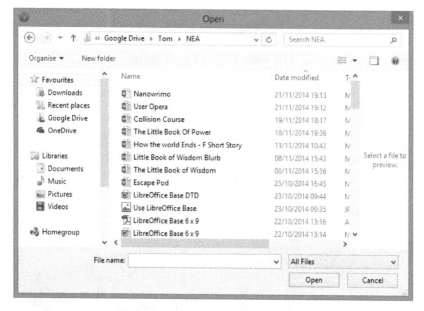

Navigate to the directory where your file is located in the normal way. Then double click on the file that you want to attach to the email.

At the bottom of the email you'll see the file name, the size of the file, then a progress bar and a cross.

User Opera.docx (5,706K)   ✕

You can cancel the upload by clicking ✕ .

When the attachment is complete you'll see:

User Opera.docx (5,706K)   ✕

You can remove the attachment by clicking ✕ . You can also open the attachment by clicking on the link (i.e. the file name which is in blue)

User Opera.docx (5,706K)

Note that you can't send the email until all attachments have uploaded.

Inserting an Image

You can insert an image from google drive (which includes drawings or photos you've made) by clicking on 🔺. This brings up a dialogue with all the pictures you've stored in google drive which is a piece of software that google uses to store information in the cloud.

It's probably more common (and, at this stage recommended) to use the upload picture facility by clicking on 📷 .

You can then go to the file you want in Windows Explorer:

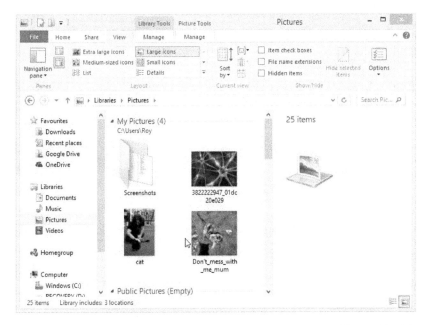

Navigate to the location where you've stored your file and hold the mouse button down, then drag it over to the Upload Photos dialogue in Opera. Move the file to the Drag Photos Here text

When you let go the attachment will automatically start to upload. While the attachment is uploading don't shut the dialogue since this may cause problems.

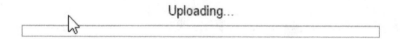

Once it's finished you'll see the picture inline with the text. This means the picture is included in the text of the email.

You can change the size of the picture by clicking on it. You can make it small, or remove the picture as well.

Note also that if you click on the picture you can resize it using the blue squares at each corner like you would in a word processor or other program. You can also align the picture using ☰ ▾ in the same way as you would using text.

Note that when you attach a picture using attachments ⬆ rather than insert image ◙ the picture isn't included in the main body of the email but instead as a piece of text in the end.

Note that when you send an email by google it automatically sends it in a format such as html which allows you to include images, formatting in text, and control the appearance. Some other email clients may use slightly different versions of html or may only show emails in plain text. Which means sometimes an email that you send will look different to someone who receives the email than the person who sent it.

You can get around this where it is very important by sending an attached document such as a pdf or word document which looks precisely how you intend it.

Most of the time the formatting that google uses will be recognised by almost all clients, and will look very similar to what you intended to send. So, this is just a warning.

Inserting a link into text

So far we've already dealt with links a lot. We've shown how we can use links to navigate web pages, open documents (see above) and even run videos.

Now, for the first time, we've reached a point in the book where we're going to add a simple link.

You can do this by typing in the text that you want the reader to read when they click the link:

Thomas Ecclestone is the author of a series of books on how to use common open source or free programs.

Then click the insert link button ⊖⊃ .

If you want a link to the web make sure ◉ **Web address** is selected. Otherwise, click on the circle next to ○ Email address .

Check that the text to display is right

Text to display: Thomas Ecclestone

If you want to link to a web page you'll enter the web address that you want to link to:

To which URL should this link refer?

thomasecclestone.co.uk|

And click on Test this link . This will open the page that you're referring to in the link.

Otherwise you'll enter the email address

To which email address should this refer?

thomasecclestone@yahoo.co.uk|

Don't worry if you get a message that says Invalid email address while you're typing the email address. Google will show it until you've got a fully formed email (as above). Note that google is only checking that the format is right. The email address itself might be wrong – i.e. go to the wrong person or be an email address that doesn't exist but is in the right format.

OK

Once you're happy with the link click .

Note that the text changes so that you've got the link in blue with an underline:

Thomas Ecclestone is the author of a series of books on how to use common open source or free programs.

If you click onto the link you can change it or remove it.

Thomas Ecclestone is the author of a series of books on how to use

Go to link:http://thomasecclestone.co.uk | Change | Remove

As you've seen already links are a very powerful tool that you can use a lot of the time. But they aren't difficult to add to an email.

Adding a smiley

A smiley or emoticon looks like☺. It's a symbol that some people use when they want to express an emotion, or to try to make sure that something that sounds harsh isn't taken too seriously.

Click on ☺ to insert a smiley.

You'll see a lot of images. At the bottom are the most common ones, such as smile, cool etc. You can insert any smiley by clicking on it. This will close the insert smiley dialogue at the same time as inserting the smiley.

Otherwise, if you hold the mouse down then click you can insert a smiley without closing the dialogue.

Check spelling

So, unless you've got immaculate spelling (which isn't my gift, I'm afraid to say!) you'll want to check the spelling before you send an email. Gmail has a spell check that is very handy for making sure that you have the spelling right.

Click on more options at the bottom right hand corner of the email and then

Check spelling ▾

This will highlight with a red underline any word that google doesn't recognise:

Thomas Ecclestone is the authore of a series of books on how to use common open source or free programs. 😊

Right click on a highlighted word to get a list of suggested words:

author

authored

authors

author e

Thoreau

Note that you can just click on a word to change the incorrect word to the correct word.

Once you've changed the email you can recheck it by clicking on  .

Printing the email

Sometimes you may want to print out a draft of an email to read it "off screen". Click on more options at the bottom right hand corner of the email and then

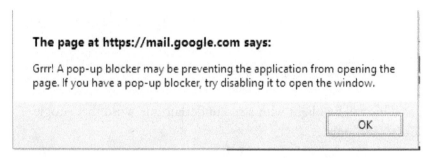

. You'll sometimes see a message saying that a popup blocker is preventing google from opening the page.

The page at https://mail.google.com says:

Grrr! A pop-up blocker may be preventing the application from opening the page. If you have a pop-up blocker, try disabling it to open the window.

OK

If this happens click on the popup blocker square next to the address bar:

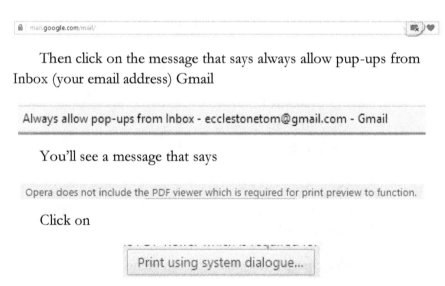

🔒 mail.google.com/mail/

Then click on the message that says always allow pup-ups from Inbox (your email address) Gmail

Always allow pop-ups from Inbox - ecclestonetom@gmail.com - Gmail

You'll see a message that says

Opera does not include the PDF viewer which is required for print preview to function.

Click on

Print using system dialogue...

This will open a preview tab. You can print it out like any other web page, clicking on ▮ Opera and then Print...   Ctrl+P . I've described the Print Settings above.

Close the preview tab by clicking on cross next to it.

This is a little bit more complicated than it would be in google chrome, but it's not too difficult to remember the steps.

Sending the email

So you've got and email written. You've checked that the To: address, cc and bcc address is right. You're happy with the message text and the attachments.

To send the email click 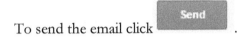 .

Checking on email that you've sent

In reading an email we've already seen the Inbox. But Gmail automatically stores every email that you send. This gives you an audit trail and allows you to prove when and to whom you sent emails. Since it's all stored on an external server it should even stand up in a court of law!

To see the email you've sent, click on sent mail under compose

This will bring up a list of mail that you've sent.

You can open an email by clicking on the subject in the same way you would in the Inbox.

Responding to an Email

When someone responds to your email

Often people will send you emails which you read and want to respond to.

When you have new, unread email google will display the number next to the inbox Inbox (1) . Click on the link and you'll see the email.

| | me, Thomas (2) | **This is a test email** - Thanks for your email, buddy! On Saturday, Nover | 10:50 |

In this case, you can see that you (me) sent the first email, and someone has responded to the email.

Click on the link.

You'll see a header including the subject, the folder, and who sent the email:

This is a test email Inbox x   thomasecclestone

Then you'll see what I call the email chain. I.e. your message to the original recipient, and any other earlier messages. You can click this to show what you've already said.

Tom Ecclestone This is some text Thomas Ecclesto 10:41 (13 minutes ago)

Then below the email chain you'll see the latest message:

 **Thomas Ecclestone**   10:50 (5 minutes ago)
to me ▾

Thanks for your email, buddy!

On Saturday, November 22, 2014 10:41 AM, Tom Ecclestone
<ecclestonetom@gmail.com> wrote:

This is some text

Gmail stores email as 'conversations' like this, so you can see what people have already read on a subject.

Responding to an email

Scroll down to the end of the email. To respond to it, click on the Reply link:

You'll see a box like the send email box. The other persons email address is already included:

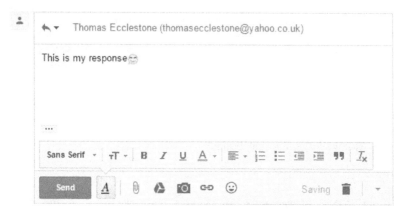

Type in the image, attach files and pictures, and change the font exactly the same way as in composing an email. When you've checked the spelling and are happy with the message click  .

If you open the link in the inbox again you'll see the conversation as follows:

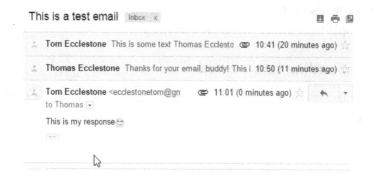

You can repeat the process as often as you like. To be honest I don't particularly enjoy talking with myself so I'll halt there!

Some more thoughts about Gmail.

While I've produced a basic guide to Gmail in this book I think there is a lot more that you can learn about it. I really chose to do a tutorial in Gmail because it sneakily teaches you things like:

- How to register an account
- How to type text, and post it
- How to add a link

But one of the problems with teaching this stuff is that the internet has an awful habit of making the same thing look very different in different applications.

For example, a link can be a piece of underlined text, or an image, or even a video clip.

When registering the form will always ask for slightly different information.

Hopefully as you read this book and use other web pages you'll recognise features you've learned from Gmail such as text fields, and post buttons, and will be able to reason things through and work out what different functionality there is.

Next Chapter

Wow, this has been a long tutorial chapter!

Hopefully you've learned a lot about how to use the internet, send an email, and register an account here. In the next chapter I'm going to go a little further.

I'm going to show you how to make a BlogSpot blog.

5 HOW TO MAKE A BLOG

So far we've been using the internet passively. What I mean by that is that we've used other people's internet sites without really creating any content ourselves. While finding out information is one of the best perks of the internet, another major perk is the ability to put your own views across.

Google provides a program that allows you to create a website for yourself which doesn't actually require much technical know-how at all.

In this chapter I'm going to show you how to make a blog using BlogSpot.

Running Blogger

First, go to google by typing its address into the address and search bar:

Log in if necessary (if the **Sign in** button is present at the top right hand corner of the screen), using the steps in the How to use Gmail account. Once you're signed in your email address should appear at the top right hand corner of the screen.

Click the apps button ⠿ near the top right hand corner of the screen to show all of googles apps.

You're looking for the following icon:

Blogger

If it isn't showing in the list of viewable icons, click More to show all the google apps. Then click the blogger icon.

You may have to enter your password when you start the new app. It depends how recently you've run google.

The first time you run Blogger you'll see a

Welcome to Blogger page.

Setting up a Profile

If you haven't created a Google Plus profile you'll be asked whether you want to create a google plus profile or a simple blogger profile.

Google plus is an application by google that provides a lot of social functionality, but explaining it is beyond the scope of this book. For this book we're only going to create a blogger profile. If you've got other knowledge of blogger you might want to create a google plus profile in which case most of the content of this chapter will still be correct.

Click on:

Create a limited Blogger profile

Then enter the name that you want to be known as

Blogger profile

Display Name | Thomas Ecclestone|

Remember that this name is very much public!

Then click Continue to Blogger .

One thing to note is that when you click the button above you're redirected to a new site:

Creating your New Blog

You'll be at the blogger help page, with a message containing your name at the top:

New Blog

To start a blog click on .

You'll see a title first. Give it the name of the blog:

Title | Use Opera User Guide

Next choose the address of your blog:

Address

UseOpera

UseOpera.blogspot.com   You can add a custom domain later.

Note that just like an email address, a BlogSpot address needs to be unique.

We've been dealing with addresses throughout the book. Because we're creating a web page we have to make a unique address that will display our page when we type it into google. If our choice is unique we will see: This blog address is available.

Out of all these steps choosing your address is the most important since you will be lumbered with it. It'll be harder to change your address later if you want to.

The final step is to choose a template. This will change how the blog looks.

Template

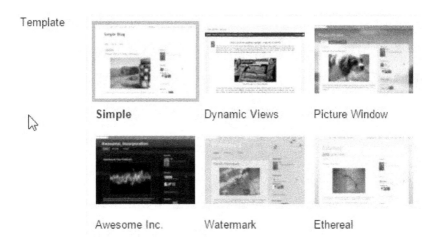

Simple   Dynamic Views   Picture Window

Awesome Inc.   Watermark   Ethereal

Just click on one that appeals. Remember that you can scroll down to see other examples.

Blogger does allow you to customise the blog a little more at a later stage, and you can also change the template. So don't worry if you're not sure about your choice.

Happy with your title, address, and theme? Then click 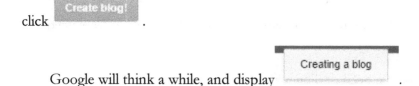 .

Google will think a while, and display  .

Once it's finished creating the blog your new blog will be listed in the welcome screen.

Clicking  at this point will open a new tab at the address you chose:

useopera.blogspot.com

Since the blog is empty it will show:

No posts found.

Content of a Blog

A blog has two main component:

- Pages
- Posts

You can think of pages as fixed content. For example, many sites have pages about the company, contact details, or similar.

Posts are dynamic, almost like a diary in reverse. Each time you post it's added to the front of the blog, and prior posts shift further down the site until they end up in an archive which people can still access. I.e. the last thing you post is the first thing that someone reads.

It's a matter of taste which you change first but as a rule I change the pages first. This is because content in pages will only rarely change so it's useful to make sure that it's okay before you write any posts.

Because you can choose different themes the appearance of the clips from here on in might be different to what you're seeing. That's normal, unfortunately, with the internet. Try to remember to think in 'concepts' rather than surface details. I know it's tough.

Managing Pages

First, log into google and Blogger (you saw how earlier in the chapter).

Next to the blog you want to add pages to is a symbol like with a down arrow next to it. Press the down arrow:

Use Opera User Guide
No posts. Start blogging!

This will bring up a series of options. Click on Pages:

You'll be taken to a webpage where you can change the pages of your blog.

Initially you probably don't have any pages.

Adding a New Page

Click on . This may take a little while, in which case you'll see a Loading... notice. Don't worry if you have to wait.

You'll notice that the page you bring up has a lot of similarities with the previous composing an email page. While the appearance is different a lot of the functionality is very similar!

The first step is to choose a Page title:

Page About Me|

Don't make the Page Title too long. Often you'll find that the Page Title becomes a link on the homepage of the site which means if it's more than a few words long it can damage the look of the site.

The next thing you'll see is an option for the type of editing you're going to do. HTML is a type of markup language that allows you to change the look of the document in a very sophisticated way. But almost always you'll want to edit using the WYSIWYG (What You See Is What You Get) mode called Compose. In other words, don't change the default setting!

Next there are a range of font buttons:

I'll explain them in a little while.

Finally there is a box where you type the text that you can find in the page:

> This is where you type your text!
>
> It's pretty cool!|

You can enter almost as much text as you like. I often like to write the text in a word processor and then copy and paste into the box.

Note that the editor has an Undo facility. If you make a mistake you can undo it using ↰ and you can redo using ↱ .

If you highlight some text you can then change the font of the text by clicking on $\mathcal{F}$ ▾ .

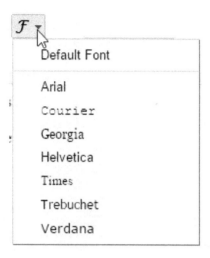

You can change the size of the text using ᵀT ▾ ,add emphasis (bold) **B** , italics *I* , underline<u>U</u> , or strike through ᴬᴮᶜ . You can change the text colour <u>A</u> ▾ or the background colour (highlight) ✎ ▾ .

In addition you can change the allignment of the text ☰ ▾ , add lists ½☰ ☰ , and quote text " . If you copy and paste text you sometimes find that you have formatting that you don't want. Highlight the text and click 𝐓ₓ to remove the formatting.

Inserting an Link

To insert a link highlight the text which you want to make into the link.

Thomas Ecclestone is an author who writes books on how to use open source software.

Click on <u>Link</u> . You'll open a link dialogue (in this case called

Edit Link).

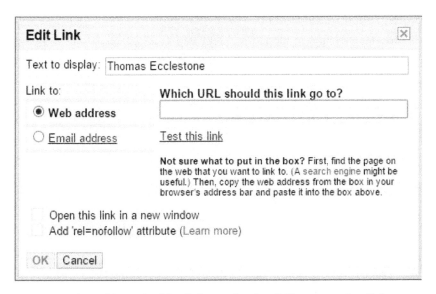

Note that although this dialogue looks different to the link dialogue in Gmail, it's actually pretty similar. You have text to display, the option of a web address or email address, a box where you include the web address (URL) and two new options.

As in the previous example type in the address you want someone to go to when they click the link:

Which URL should this link go to?

thomasecclestone.co.uk

Or the email address if you select that option:

Which email address should this link to?

thomasecclestone@yahoo.co.uk

You can ~~Test this link~~ if you want to.

There are, however, two new options. If you select

Open this link in a new window by clicking on the square the link will open a new web tab when you click it. So you won't leave your website open. If you select

Add 'rel=nofollow' attribute (Learn more) you add an attribute to the link that tells the search engine that you don't want it to take into account the fact you've linked to the web page when it works out what position in google search the page should be.

I tend to suggest leaving these two alone, unless for some reason you don't think that the site you're linking to is a good one. In which case you'd click Add 'rel=nofollow' attribute (Learn more) .

Once you're happy click OK .

Thomas Ecclestone is an author who writes books on how to use open source software.

One of the interesting things about this is that although the web dialogue *looks* different than the previous example of an add link dialogue the actual things you need to enter are very similar. You'll see this often in web sites.

Inserting an Image

Go to the point in the page where you want to insert the image and then click .

You'll see an insert picture dialogue. There are a lot of options but in this book I'm just going to show you how to insert an image from a file.

Click on Upload .

Then on Choose files .

This will bring an Open dialogue up. Navigate to the correct directory and double click on a picture to insert it:

You may upload multiple files at once. Use JPG, GIF or PNG files.

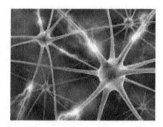

You can then single click on the picture in the Upload dialogue:

You may upload multiple files at once. Use JPG, GIF or PNG files.

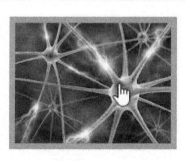

And click on **Add selected** .

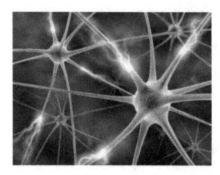

It's pretty cool!

Thomas Ecclestone is an author who writes books on how to use open source software.

Note that you can drag the image around the page by selecting it and moving it with the mouse.

If you click on the image you can chose what size it should be, align it, and add a caption or even remove it.

Small - Medium - Large - X-Large - Original size | Left - Centre - Right | Add caption | Properties | Remove [x]

Inserting an Video

Go to the place in the Page where you want to insert the video and click on 🎬 .

From a file

Upload

Click ———— and then drag the video over from file explorer to the text:

Drag video here

You'll see:

Videos can take quite a while to upload so don't worry if it seems to be taking a long time!

From YouTube

In the Insert Video dialogue you opened earlier click on From YouTube.

You will find a YouTube search box. This is almost exactly the same as a google search except it'll search only YouTube!

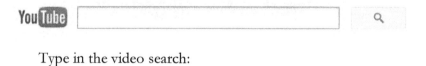

Type in the video search:

And press enter. Google will show some videos@

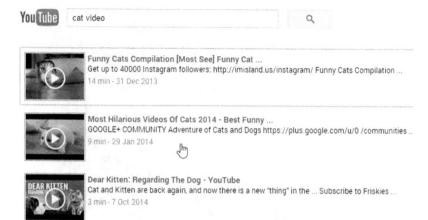

Double click on the one that you want to include. Note that when you're using YouTube videos, inserting the video is very quick since it's already been uploaded for you:

That's it. You've uploaded the video! When someone wants to play it they'll just press

Spell Checking

This works just the same way as in Gmail. Click and Blogger

will highlight your errors. You can right click on an error to get suggestions.

Save an Draft

You don't have to write everything at once. You can

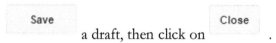

a draft, then click on .

Note that in the Pages dialogue your new page will be shown, but will have the word Draft by it.

Click on the page title (e.g. in this case About Me) to open the page for editing.

Preview

Click on Preview to bring up a new tab that will show you exactly what the page that you're editing will look like.

Publish

Click on Publish to publish the page that you're working to the internet.

Delete a Page

Before you start it's important to realise that if you delete a post you will not be able to change your mind later. Click on the square next to the post name to select the post.

Then click on Delete .

A warning dialogue will appear:

Are you sure that you want to delete the selected page(s)?

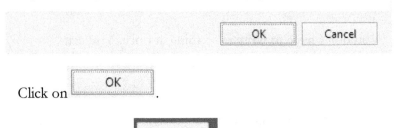

Click on .

Blogger will display and the page will be removed from the list of posts.

New Post

Click on from the My Blogs page, or alternatively

 if you are already in your blog.

Actually entering the text of the blog is very similar to adding a page. First, you type in your title:

Leave the editor method alone .

Type in the text that you want in your post:

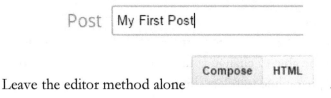

Highlight text and add links, change the format, insert images or videos etc. in the same way as Adding a New Page above:

And even save, preview, and publish in the same way:

So, what's different from adding a page above? The main thing is that a post can have settings. These affect how you can find the post (Labels), when the post will appear (Schedule), whether the post will have a permanent link or not (Permalink), Location and other options.

The two most useful features in this is the Schedule and Label feature, so I'll describe them here.

Adding Labels

A label is a word (or a couple of words) that describes a post. Users can search the blog by labels, and see all posts on a particular theme.

To add labels click on Labels in the post settings

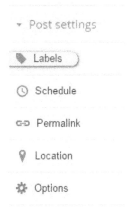

And type in the labels you want for the blog with each label separated by a comma:

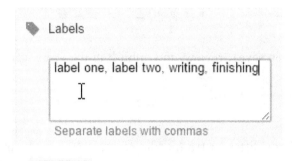

Then click **Done**. You'll see the labels you've chosen under the Labels setting. Note that I generally recommend thinking a little about what labels you use for common themes or subjects of your blog since it's important to keep related themes together rather than use a different label for the same subject.

🏷 Labels

label one, label two, writing, finishing

Scheduling a Post

It's useful to be able to store posts until a time in the future so that you can go on holiday without having to worry about your blog.

To schedule click on 🕐 Schedule in the Settings options.

Then on the circle next to set date and time ⬭ Set date and time .

You can type the date and time into the boxes:

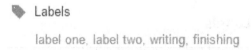

24 Nov 2014   06:49

or click on the calendar.

Note that if you set a date in the past the post will display as being posted on the date you set. If you set it in the future the post won't be public until the time you've scheduled it to appear.

Some Thoughts

In this chapter I've obviously only included the very basics of Blogger. You can change the appearance, monetize (i.e. make money from the blog) and do many other things with it. But I think that the information in this chapter and the prior chapter on search ought to at least get you started being an active participant on the internet.

So Long!

I've really enjoyed showing you how to use Opera, the free internet browser to speed up your web browsing, search google, look at videos, and even start up your own web blog.

One of the problems with a subject so vast as this is that there's always something else to learn… which is one of the reasons I started with Search! Because that'll help you to learn everything that I've inevitably missed from a beginners guide.

I hope that you enjoy the freedom that Opera can bring you.

If you have any questions feel free to email thomasecclestone@yahoo.co.uk and until then thank you for reading the book!

I hope you have fun on the internet.

!

ABOUT THE AUTHOR

Thomas Ecclestone is a software engineer and technical writer who lives in Kent, England. After getting his 1st class honours in software engineering he worked at the National Computing Centre in Manchester, the Manchester Metropolitan University, and for BEC systems Integration before starting his own business in software development. He is a writer who lives on a smallholding in Kent where he looks after a small flock of Hebridean sheep.

www.ingramcontent.com/pod-product-compliance
Lightning Source LLC
Chambersburg PA
CBHW071003050326
40689CB00014B/3467